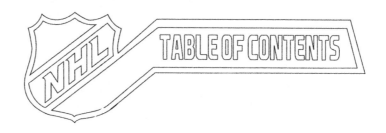

TABLE OF CONTENTS

players

logos

design center

NICKLAS
BACKSTROM

NICKLAS
BACKSTROM

JAMIE
BENN

JAMIE
BENN

PATRICE
BERGERON

PATRICE
BERGERON

BRENT
BURNS

BRENT
BURNS

5

DUSTIN BYFUGLIEN

DUSTIN BYFUGLIEN

DREW DOUGHTY

DREW
DOUGHTY

8

JOHNNY GAUDREAU

RYAN
GETZLAF

TURN BOOK SIDEWAYS TO COLOR

RYAN GETZLAF

TURN BOOK SIDEWAYS TO COLOR

MARK GIORDANO

CLAUDE GIROUX

CLAUDE GIROUX

TAYLOR
HALL

TAYLOR
HALL

VICTOR
HEDMAN

VICTOR
HEDMAN

14

BRADEN
HOLTBY

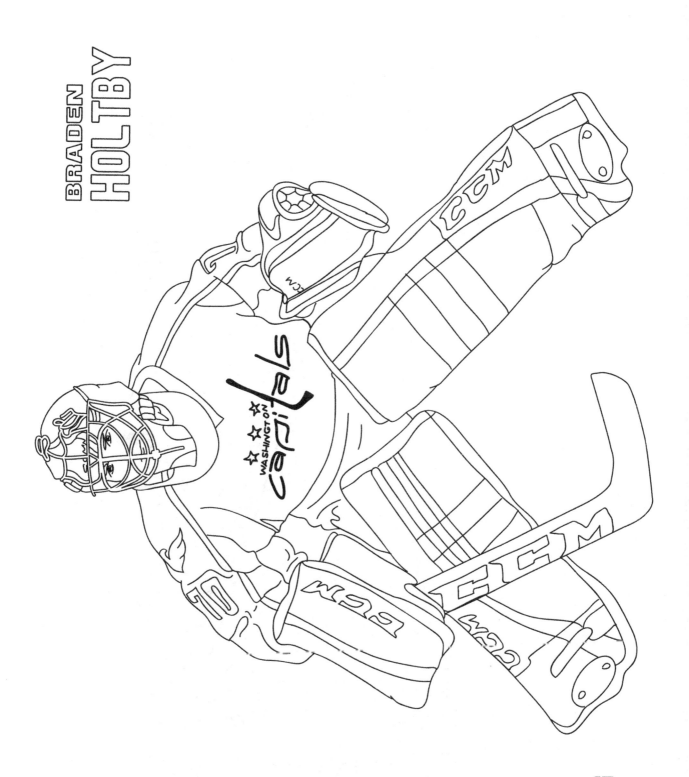

15

PATRICK
KANE

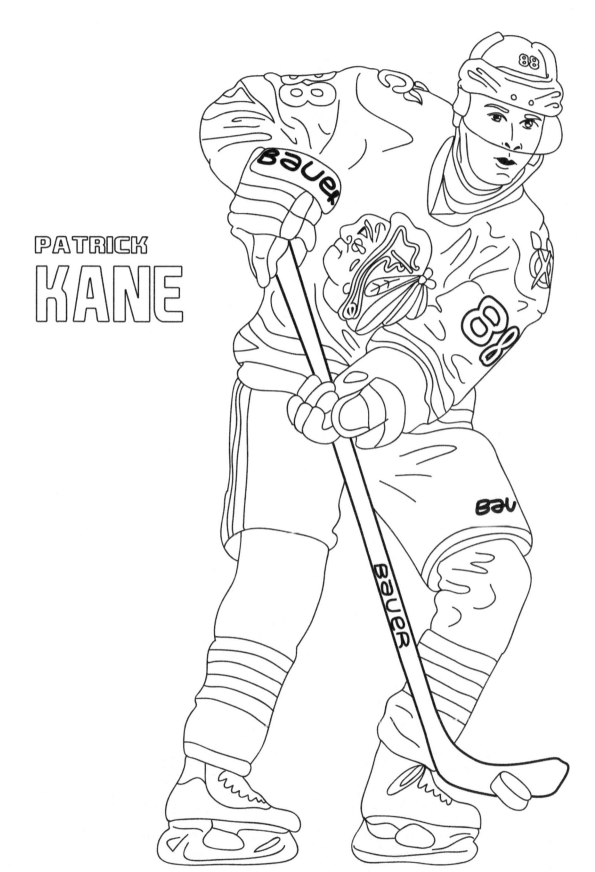

PATRICK
KANE

16

ERIK
KARLSSON

ERIK
KARLSSON

17

DUNCAN
KEITH

DUNCAN
KEITH

18

ANZE
KOPITAR

ANZE
KOPITAR

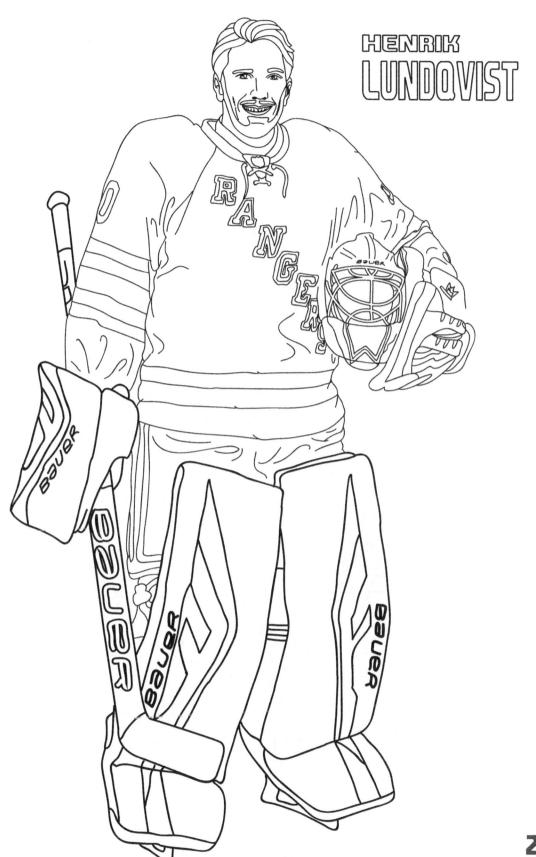

HENRIK
LUNDQVIST

20

EVGENI MALKIN

CONNOR
MCDAVID

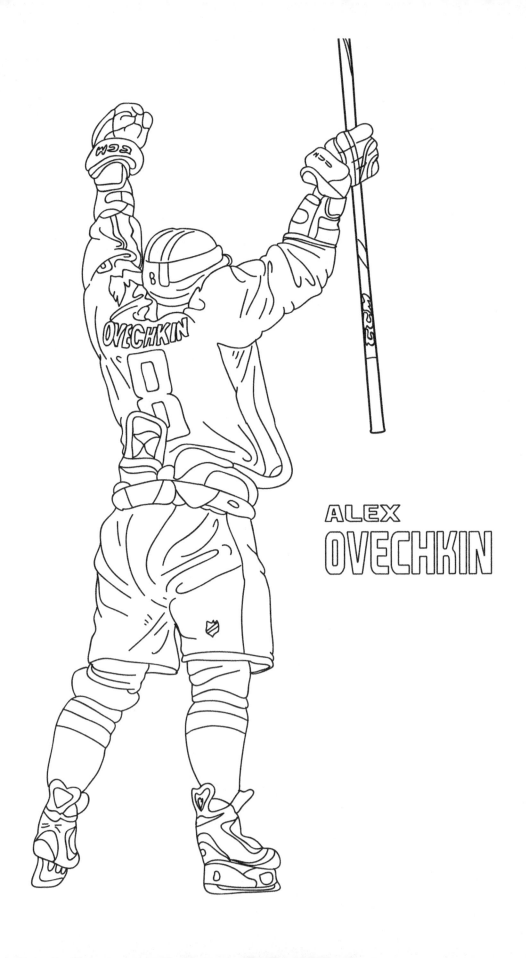

ALEX
OVECHKIN

ALEX
OVECHKIN

23

JOE PAVELSKI

JOE PAVELSKI

COREY
PERRY

COREY
PERRY

CAREY
PRICE

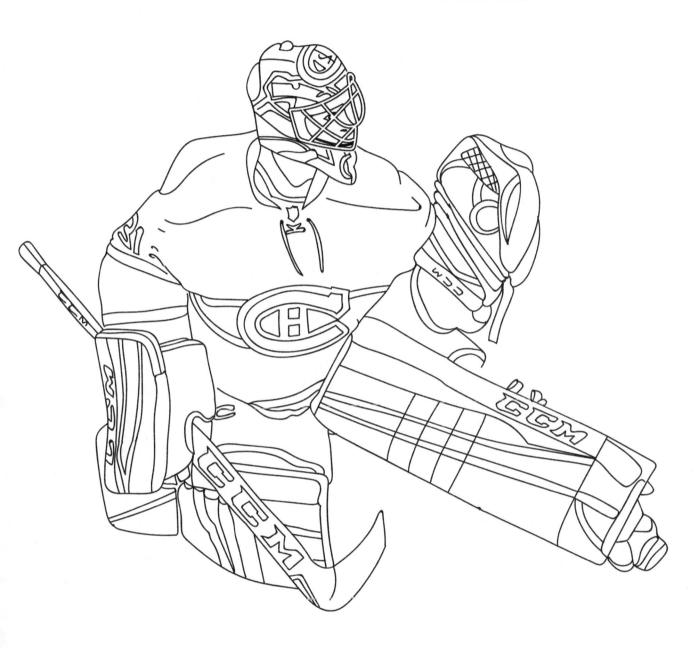

JONATHAN
QUICK

TYLER
SEGUIN

TYLER
SEGUIN

28

STEVEN STAMKOS

STEVEN STAMKOS

RYAN
SUTER

VLADIMIR
TARASENKO

VLADIMIR
TARASENKO

JOHN TAVARES

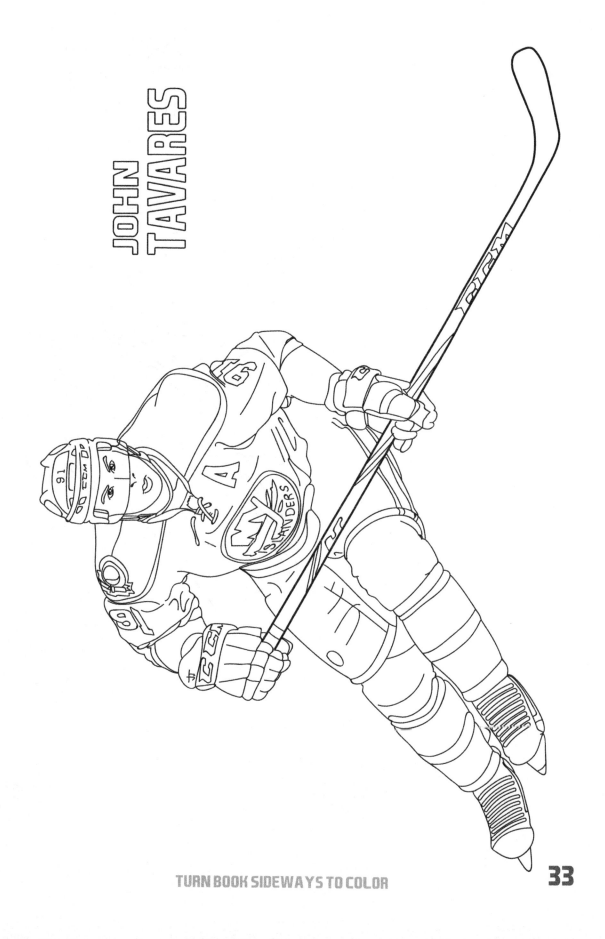

JOHN TAVARES

JONATHAN
TOEWS

MARC EDOUARD VLASIC

VLASIC

TURN BOOK SIDEWAYS TO COLOR

MARC EDOUARD VLASIC

JAKUB
VORACEK

JAKUB
VORACEK

SHEA
WEBER

SHEA
WEBER

NHL TEAMS

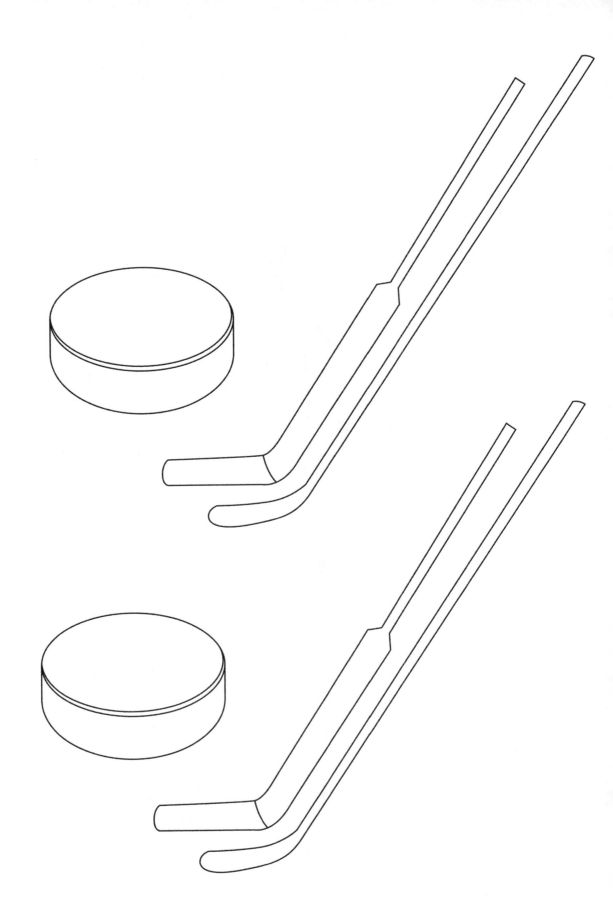

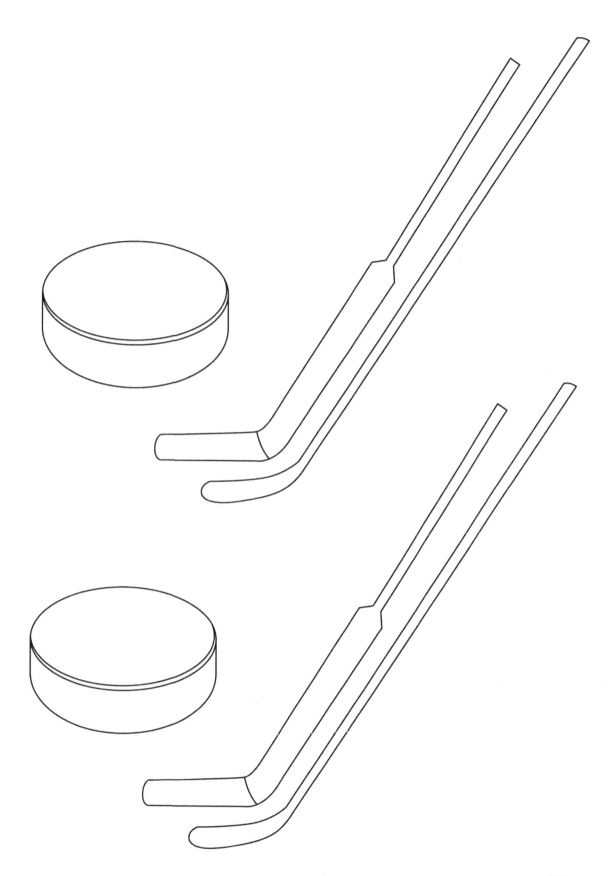

44

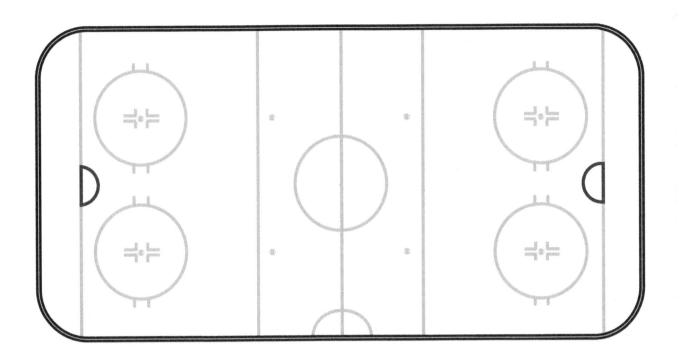

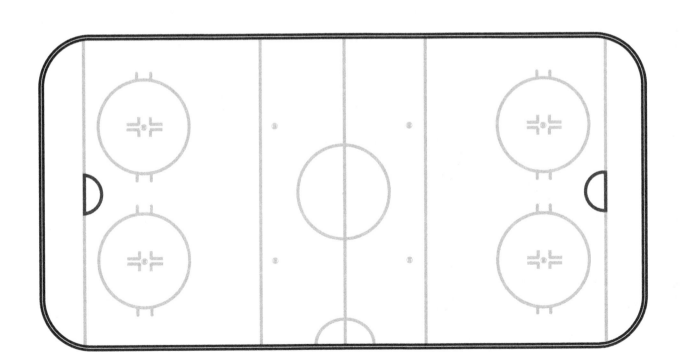

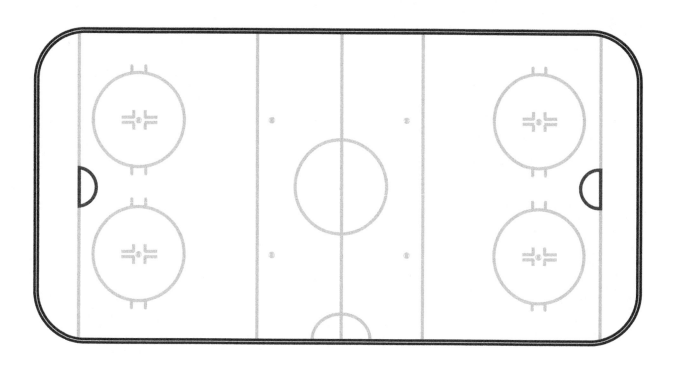

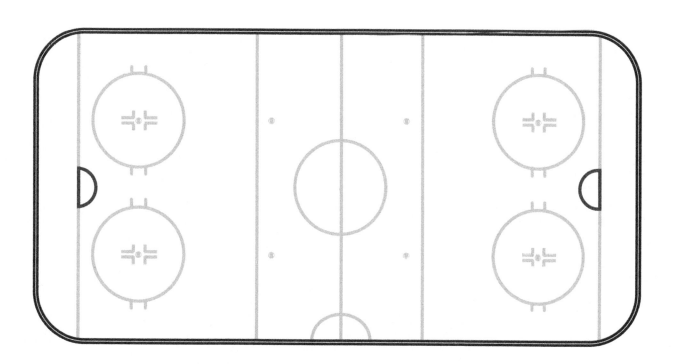

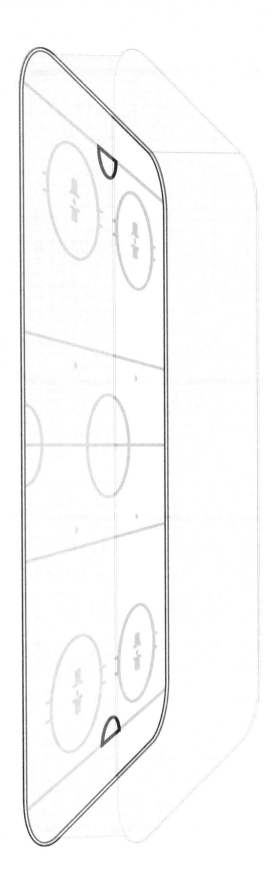

Turn book sideways to color your favorite players and fans in action!

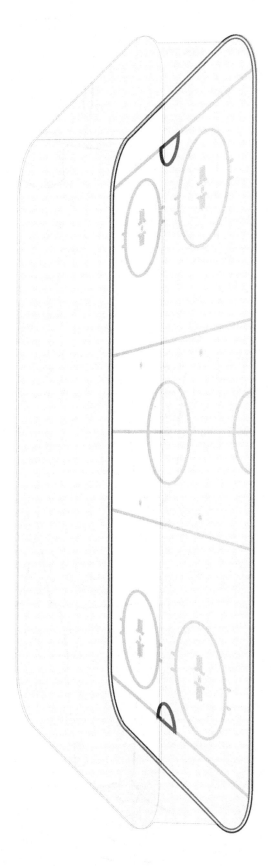

Turn book sideways to color your favorite players and fans in action! **46**

Made in the USA
Middletown, DE
29 May 2023

31696497R00057